ISBN 978-1-330-96025-7
PIBN 10126658

This book is a reproduction of an important historical work. Forgotten Books uses state-of-the-art technology to digitally reconstruct the work, preserving the original format whilst repairing imperfections present in the aged copy. In rare cases, an imperfection in the original, such as a blemish or missing page, may be replicated in our edition. We do, however, repair the vast majority of imperfections successfully; any imperfections that remain are intentionally left to preserve the state of such historical works.

1 MONTH OF
FREE
READING

at

www.ForgottenBooks.com

By purchasing this book you are
eligible for one month membership to
ForgottenBooks.com, giving you
unlimited access to our entire
collection of over 1,000,000 titles via
our web site and mobile apps.

To claim your free month visit:

www.forgottenbooks.com/free126658

English
Français
Deutsche
Italiano
Español
Português

www.forgottenbooks.com

Mythology Photography **Fiction**
Fishing Christianity **Art** Cooking
Essays Buddhism Freemasonry
Medicine **Biology** Music **Ancient
Egypt** Evolution Carpentry Physics
Dance Geology **Mathematics** Fitness
Shakespeare **Folklore** Yoga Marketing
Confidence Immortality Biographies
Poetry **Psychology** Witchcraft
Electronics Chemistry History **Law**
Accounting **Philosophy** Anthropology
Alchemy Drama Quantum Mechanics
Atheism Sexual Health **Ancient History**
Entrepreneurship Languages Sport
Paleontology Needlework Islam
Metaphysics Investment Archaeology
Parenting Statistics Criminology
Motivational

The Fantasticks

A ROMANTIC COMEDY *in Three Acts by* EDMOND ROSTAND

Freely Done into *English Verse by* GEORGE FLEMING

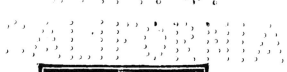

BY THE SAME AUTHOR

Uniform with this Volume

CYRANO DE BERGERAC

A Play in Five Acts

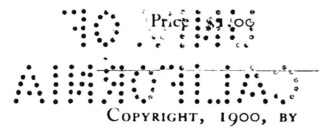

Price $1.00

PERSONS OF THE PLAY

PERCINET	. . . .	A Lover
STRAFOREL	. . . .	A Bravo
BERGAMIN	. . . .	Father to Percinet
PASQUIN	. . . .	Father to Sylvette
BLAISE	. . . . .	A Gardener
SYLVETTE	. . . .	{ Daughter of Pasquin { in love with Percinet

BRAVOS, MUSICIANS, NEGROES, TORCH-BEARERS, A NOTARY, WITNESSES, WEDDING-GUESTS, etc.

——— ———

The Scene to take place where one pleases, provided the Costumes are pretty enough

THIS VERSION OF

" LES ROMANTIQUES "

WAS FIRST PRODUCED AT THE ROYALTY THEATRE

MAY 29, 1900

THE FANTASTICKS

ACT I

The stage is divided by an old mossy wall covered with climbing plants and vines. To the right a bit of BERGAMIN'S *park; to the left the park belonging to* PASQUIN. *Benches against the wall on either side.*

The curtain rising discloses PERCINET *seated on the top of the wall, with a book on his knee. He is reading aloud to* SYLVETTE, *who listens attentively from the other side of the wall, against which she leans, standing on the bench L.*

SYLVETTE
[*clasping her hands in admiration, and looking at* PERCINET].

How beautiful! how beautiful! dear Percinet,—
[*she checks herself, looks down, and adds shyly*]
—dear friend.

PERCINET
[*with enthusiasm, but absorbed in his book*].

Wait till you hear the lovely, perfect end!
Now, Romeo: [*He reads.*] 'Look, love, what envious streaks

' Do lace the severing clouds in yonder east ;
' Night's candles are burnt out, and jocund day
' Stands tiptoe on the misty mountain-top ':

[*With expression.*]

' I must be gone and live ; or stay and——'

SYLVETTE

[*who has been listening to some imaginary sound,
interrupts him sharply*].

Stop !

Listen !　[*She looks about in alarm.*]

PERCINET

[*after listening*].

No !—nothing to be seen or heard.

[*Half tender, half bantering*].

Sylvia ! your heart is like a little bird
That flutters from her nest if leaves but stir.
Cease trembling, Faintheart !　[*Takes up book.*]
　　　　　　　　　Listen now to Her—
That Juliet, whose love could never die.

[*He reads.*]

' Yon light is not daylight, I know it, I ;
' It is some meteor that the sun exhales
' To be to thee this night a torch-bearer.' . . .
Then He :—' Yon grey is not the morning's eye,
' 'Tis but the pale reflex of Cynthia's brow ;
' Nor that is not the lark whose notes do beat

' The vaulty heaven so high above our heads :
' I have more care to stay than will to go.'

[*He looks up and speaks with emotion.*]

' Come, death, and welcome ! Juliet wills it so !'

SYLVETTE

[*childishly*].

No, no !—not *that*.   Oh ! do not let him die !
If you go on, I 'll—weep.

PERCINET

[*turning to her with a sudden smile*].

I would not have you cry.
And, since my lady's pleasure sits that way,

[*He looks at his book, and shuts it.*]

Let noble Romeo live another day.

[*He looks about him.*]

How the leaves rustle !   How those great boughs
seem
Bending and brooding over Shakespeare's dream !

SYLVETTE.

Yes ; they are beautiful, enchanted speeches :
I love them too.   And all these waving beeches
Sway to their rhythm in a mood divine.
O yes, I, too, have found your Shakespeare fine.
Only, [*naïvely*] his verse is finer, Percinet,
When *you* recite it.   For—you have a way——

PERCINET

[*delighted, but protesting*].

Flatterer!

SYLVETTE

[*nodding her head gravely*].

A certain way of saying certain things—
[*She sighs.*]
But those poor lovers——
[*Mournfully.*]
Ah, what sufferings!
[*She sighs.*]
They make me think——

PERCINET

[*quickly*].

Of whom?

SYLVETTE

[*blushing, embarrassed*].

Oh!—no one whom one knows.

PERCINET

[*half teasing*].

And is that why your face becomes a rose?

SYLVETTE

[*putting her hands to her cheeks*].

No one!

PERCINET.

Ah, Sylvia!

[*Threatening her with his finger.*]
                    Those transparent eyes
Can hide no secrets—save of Paradise.

[*Mysteriously.*]
Our own two fathers you remembered then.

SYLVETTE.

Perhaps I did.

PERCINET.

Two angry, worthy men,
Whom long hate sunders——

SYLVETTE.

                    And hate *can* divide.
When I've remembered that [*sadly*] I've—very
                              often—cried.
For when I first grew up—a whole long month ago—
And left my convent's shade to see the great
                              world's show,

[*she waves her hands towards the trees, etc.*]
My father brought me here, beside these mossy
                              stones,
And showed me, over there, the park *your* father
                              owns.
'Look, child,' he said, 'yon fair wood is the den
Where lurks my mortal foe, the worst of living
                              men—

A certain Master Bergamin, whose son
Must *never* cross thy path.—I bid thee shun
All sight, all contact with that loathèd name.
Thy hate and mine must show an equal flame,
Or I renounce thee.   Promise !—or be cursed !'
                    [*Solemnly.*]
I promised.   [*With a change of voice.*]   But I had
                              not seen you first !

                    PERCINET.

And did I not the same mad oath repeat ?
I swore to hate you.   And—I love you, Sweet.

                    SYLVETTE
                    [*starting back*].
Love *me* ?

                    PERCINET
                    [*firmly*].
        I love you.

                    SYLVETTE
                    [*faltering*].
              But—that is a crime.

                    PERCINET
              [*grandiloquently*].
It is.   What matter ?   *Every* single time
Love is forbid, love seeks some swifter way.
                    [*Violently.*]
I love you.—Kiss me.

SYLVETTE.

Fie, fie, Percinet!

[*She jumps down from the bench and runs away.*]

PERCINET

[*with reproachful surprise*].

And yet—you love me.

SYLVETTE

[*scandalised*].

Oh!

PERCINET.

But, dearest child,
I put your thought in words.   We were beguiled
If we still doubted.   ·What I speak, you've said.
You said it, Sylvia.   *You* compared the dead
Immortal lovers of Verona——

SYLVETTE

[*putting her hands to her ears*].

No!

PERCINET.

—To us, my Juliet!—*I* am Romeo.

SYLVETTE.

I never did compare——

PERCINET.

Our battling fathers, Sweet,
Remember them.   And see me at thy feet,
O fairer Juliet!—Brother Montagu,
          [*stretching out his arms*]
You had the old love; have I not the new?
     [*With emphasis, turning to* SYLVETTE.]
Well as they loved, I'll love you better yet,
Right in the teeth of Father Capulet.

SYLVETTE

[*drawing a little nearer the wall*].
But *are* we lovers?   Can love be so swift?

PERCINET

Love never bargains o'er his royal gift.
I watched you pass my door——

SYLVETTE

[*naïvely*].

And I saw too.

PERCINET

Our eyes had spoken ere your name I knew.

SYLVETTE

One day I looked for nuts beside this wall;
It was by chance——

PERCINET.

By chance—no plan at all—
I brought my book, and——

SYLVETTE.

Off my ribbon blew.

PERCINET.

What man controls his fate? I guessed 'twas
You.
I climbed this bench to seize the precious knot——

SYLVETTE

[*getting up on the bench*].

I climbed this bench——

PERCINET.

And by this blessèd spot
I wait each day, with beating heart, to hear
The music of your bird-laugh drawing near.
Your laugh—your signal. Then your dear hair
shines,
And your dear face uprises through the vines.

SYLVETTE.

Since we are lovers, we should plight our troth.

PERCINET.

I've thought of that.

SYLVETTE.

I, Sylvette, nothing loath—
Last of the Pasquinots—to you, the last
Of all the Bergamins——

[*She holds out her hand, which he kisses.*]

PERCINET.

I 'll hold my treasure fast !

SYLVETTE.

People will talk of Us in years and years to be.

PERCINET.

Two tender blossoms of too harsh a tree !

SYLVETTE.

And yet, who knows, dear friend ?   The hour may
                                                                ring
When Heaven, through us, may soothe their
                                                            bickering.

PERCINET.

I doubt it !

SYLVETTE.

But I *feel* that Fate befriends.
Besides,—I 've thought of half a dozen ends
All possible, and——

PERCINET.

What ?

SYLVETTE.

But, dearest, only look !
Suppose—I 've read of such things in a book—
Suppose a prince—that prince who never fails !—
Should ride this way, as in the fairy tales ?
—I fly to tell him of our hopeless love :
He listens : I beseech.   All other men above,
A prince gives orders ; and our fathers' pride
Bends to his will——

PERCINET.

They give me You for bride—.

SYLVETTE.

Or,—as in dear old Beauty and the Beast,—
You seem to sicken,—you grow pale, at least—.

PERCINET.

My trembling father bids me name my care,——

SYLVETTE.

You say, ' I die, since Sylvia is so fair ! '

PERCINET.

His heart *must* soften !

SYLVETTE.

Or—another plan :—
Some rich old Duke, some old and wicked man,
Who sees my portrait, sends to me a page
All golden armour, to demand some gage
That I become his Duchess.

PERCINET.

[*interrupting*].

But you answer 'No!'

SYLVETTE.

Then, on a night, as is my wont, I go
Deep in the park's dim shade, to dream of Thee.
His minions seize me; then I shriek——

PERCINET.

For Me!

I fly—my dagger in my vengeful hand—
And, like a lion, leap upon their band——

SYLVETTE.

Three—four men sink before your flashing blade;—
Enters my father; hails you; unafraid
You tell your noble name; he bursts in tears of
joy;
And, when he yields his Girl, your father gives
his Boy.

PERCINET.

And ever after that, we live in perfect bliss.

SYLVETTE

[*seriously*].

Dearest, there's nothing surely very strange in
this?

PERCINET

[*hearing a noise*].

Somebody coming!

SYLVETTE
[*losing her head*].

Kiss me !

PERCINET.

Till to-night.

You will return at dusk ?

SYLVETTE.

No.

PERCINET.

Yes,—my Heart's Delight !

SYLVETTE
[*disappearing behind the wall*].

Your father !
[PERCINET *leaps nimbly down from the wall.*]

BERGAMIN.
[SYLVETTE *is invisible where he stands.*]

What ! I find you mooning here ?
Always in this same spot ?

PERCINET.

But this spot is so dear !
I love this spot. I love this mossy seat :
See how the wild vines clasp its faithful feet !
See how, in arabesques, their tendrils fall !—
The air tastes sweeter here.

BERGAMIN.

Here ?   By this stifling wall ?

PERCINET

[*with enthusiasm*].

I love that wall !

BERGAMIN.

I 'm sure I can't see why.

SYLVETTE

[*aside*].

He cannot see.

PERCINET

[*with a touch of fatuity*].

But, sir, you won't deny
Its beauty ?   See that happy crown of grass ;—
The redd'ning vines mix with the ivy's green ;—
With pale wisteria ; and the paler mass
Of honeyed woodbine and of eglantine.
My fine old wall ! that from its gaping sides
Flings to the sun a strange and ruddy fleece
All starred with gentle flowers ; whose deep moss
                                        hides
This bench, whereon a king might rest at ease.

BERGAMIN.

Tut ! tut ! young man.—That cock won't fight at
                                        all.—
You 'd have me think you make eyes at *a wall* ?

PERCINET
[*same manner*].
But, father! when a wall has flower-eyes!
[*He turns to the wall and addresses* SYLVETTE
out of sight.]
*E*yes like blue stars!—*E*yes of the right June-blue.
Smiles of pure azure.—Looks of blue surprise.
—As if some flower should learn the way to woo.
[*With emotion.*] By Heaven! if e'er I should forget
their power——

BERGAMIN
[*shouting*].
*W*alls—have—no—*eyes* !

PERCINET.
What do you call--this flower ?
[*Smiling and foppish, he offers* BERGAMIN *a*
flower he deftly picks from the wall.]

SYLVETTE
[*aside*].
Sweet heaven! how clever!

BERGAMIN
[*with a grunt, after staring at him and his flower*].
Son, you are—an Ass.
But well I know what's brought you to this pass.
[*Signs of alarm from* PERCINET *and* SYLVETTE.]

You hide away—to read.

[*He snatches the book from* PERCINET'S *pocket,*
and looks at it.]

Plays !

[*He opens book and lets it fall with horror.*]

O Lord !—*Poetry.*

Written in verse,—in verse.   Dear Lord ! can
such things be ?

[*Pointing each word with his stick on the ground.*]

You moon—you hide—ignore your neighbour's
needs ;

You talk of eyes, and walls, pick foolish weeds ;—
*E*yes in my wall ! — Good God !   [*Mimicking*
PERCINET.]   *E*yes ! mosses ! flowers ! Fate !
[*Shouting.*]   Walls—have—no—eyes, my lad.
They need to be built—straight.

[*Pointing to wall with stick.*]

Who knows what threat'ning breach may lurk
behind that screen ?

I 'll send my men, anon, to strip yon silly
green.

To keep a hated neighbour well at bay,
I 'll have that whole side whitewashed.   All the
way

I 'll set it thick with sharp and broken glass,
Fragments of bottles, till no fly may pass
My rankèd legions——

PERCINET.

Father, spare my vines—!

BERGAMIN.

Not one.   All glass.   All razor-cutting lines.

PERCINET *and* SYLVETTE
[*overcome with horror*].

Oh!

BERGAMIN.

But to business.   [*He sits on the bench R.*]
Hm-m?   [*He gets up, looks at
wall suspiciously.*]
Though walls can't *see,*
They've ears can hear.
[*He appears to be about to climb the bench.   Alarm of
PERCINET.   SYLVETTE, on hearing the noise,
makes herself as small as possible and crouches
under the wall.   But BERGAMIN, making a
face which shows he is suffering from some old
stiffness, beckons to his son to climb in his stead
and look over.   To PERCINET.*]
You climb, and look for me.
[*PERCINET scrambles quickly on the bench, leans
over the wall and speaks to SYLVETTE, who
has immediately risen.*]

PERCINET
[*to SYLVETTE*].

To-night?—To-night?

SYLVETTE

[*giving him her hand, which he kisses ; in a low voice*].

I 'll come.   As soon as darkness nears.

PERCINET

[*same voice*].

I shall be here.

SYLVETTE

[*same voice*].

I love you.

BERGAMIN.

Well ?

PERCINET

[*jumping down lightly ; aloud*].

No sign of—ears !

BERGAMIN

[*reassured, sits down again*].

Then business, son.   I 've chosen you a wife.

SYLVETTE.

Ah !

BERGAMIN.

What was that ?

PERCINET.

That ?   Nothing.

BERGAMIN.

'Pon my life,
I swear I heard a cry.

PERCINET
[*looking up into the trees*].
Some little wounded bird—.

SYLVETTE.

Alas !

PERCINET.

I almost think the branch above there stirred—.

BERGAMIN.

Well then, my only son, with due reflection
ripe
I've made your choice——

PERCINET
[*moves away up stage, whistling impertinently*].
Whew ! Whew !

BERGAMIN
[*after an instant of suffocating indignation
follows him*].
Whistle ! you silly snipe !
I am not to be moved.

PERCINET

[*with impertinence, coming down stage*].

Whew-ew!

BERGAMIN.

You—piping merle!
I say, I've made your choice.   I've found your
                                    wife.   A pearl.

PERCINET.

And—if I don't like pearls?

BERGAMIN

[*stupefied*].

Not—*like*?   God bless my soul,
[*he raises his cane*] I'll teach you what you like——
[PERCINET *wards off the stick with his hand.*]

BERGAMIN.

You scamp! you——

PERCINET

[*calmly, sentimentally*].

                              Sir, the whole
Green coppice is alive with spring-awakened
                                    song;
And where young leaves are thick, young birds
                              woo all day long
By little woodland streams——

BERGAMIN.

Indecent !

PERCINET

[*same business, with stick*].

It is May.
The world is full of laughter.   Flies, at play——

BERGAMIN.

Profligate !

PERCINET

[*same business*].

——swarm, in sunny fields, to kiss
The   thousand   flowers,   whose   opening   makes
their bliss.
For Love——

BERGAMIN.

You—bandit !

PERCINET.

——sets all hearts a-quake.
——And you would have *me* wed for reason's sake ?

BERGAMIN

[*with rage*].

You shall, you scoundrel !

PERCINET

[*very sweetly*].

My—de-ar—father,—no.

Dear wall! [*turning towards* SYLVETTE] bear
witness that it is not so.

For when I wed, I'll wed such high romance
As never yet was seen on sea or land—.

[*To* BERGAMIN.]

Before I yield, I'll lead you such a dance——

[*Runs off stage.   Exit.*]

BERGAMIN.

Wait till I catch you!

[*Runs after* PERCINET, *brandishing stick.   Exit.*]

SYLVETTE

[*looking after* BERGAMIN].

Oh! I understand
Almost—my papa's hate for this old——

PASQUIN

[*entering L.*].

Well?

And what is Missy doing?

SYLVETTE

[*quickly*].

I'll not tell!

[*Confused.*]

—Nothing!—I mean—I'm walking—.

PASQUIN.

Tut! tut! careless maid,
How came you all alone? And *here*?

SYLVETTE
[*hurriedly*].

I 'm not afraid.

PASQUIN.

Alone? Beside this wall? But I forbade you,
child,
Ever to see this wall.—What! will you drive
me wild?
Have you forgot this park, this haunt, this horrid
den
Where lurks my oldest foe—the worst of living
men?

SYLVETTE
[*rather bored*].

I know, papa.

PASQUIN.

And yet you linger by this wall.—
You dare their evil looks.—You take no pains
at all!—
What if this ruffian's son — fit son of ruffian
sire,—
Should find *my* daughter here, frail victim to
his ire?

The bare thought makes me creep.—Quick,
quick ! with iron nails
Let me beset this wall ;—with sharp and cutting
flails ;—
I 'll turn it to a knife ; a porcupine ; a spear ;
I 'll make my iron bite each mortal thing that 's
near ;
I 'll bristle like a boar——

SYLVETTE
[*aside*].
Until he counts the cost !
Papa 's no spendthrift.

PASQUIN.
Go !—[*Tenderly*] Mind that you don't get lost.
[*Exit* SYLVETTE.   *He watches her out of sight
with affected anger.*]
[*Enter* BERGAMIN, *speaking off stage.*]

BERGAMIN.
This note, post haste, to Master Straforel.

PASQUIN
[*running to the wall and climbing the bench L.*].
Bergamin !

BERGAMIN
[*same business, bench R.*].
Pasquin !
[*They embrace.*]

PASQUIN
[*affectionately*].
　　Do I see you well ?

BERGAMIN.
So, so, old friend.

PASQUIN
[*solicitous*].
That gout ?

BERGAMIN
[*shrugs shoulders*].
　　Ugh !　But *you* had a cough ?

PASQUIN.
I have one.　[*Coughs.*]

BERGAMIN
[*rubbing his hands*].
　　Well, 'tis done.　That marriage will
　　　　　　　　come off !

PASQUIN.
What ?

BERGAMIN.
　　Oh, I heard it all.　I hid there [*pointing*]
　　　　　　　　by those trees.
They 're mad—quite mad—with love.

PASQUIN.

Hurray !

BERGAMIN

[*same business, rubbing hands*].

Mad as you please.
To business now—ha! ha!—and that right
speedily.
——Two fathers, and two cheery widowers, we;
I had one son, of a romantic name——

PASQUIN.

Fantastic !

BERGAMIN

[*with a shrug*].

His poor mother pined for fame—.
You had one daughter — sky-blue — with a
Soul.
—What was our hope ?   What was our daily
goal ?

PASQUIN.

To overthrow this wall.

BERGAMIN.

To live here, side by side.

PASQUIN.

To join the two estates——

BERGAMIN.

Like old friends, true and tried——

PASQUIN.

Like prudent landlords, too——

BERGAMIN.

For that, what did we plan ?

PASQUIN.

Our children's marriage ; hey ?

BERGAMIN.

But think, my dear old man :
If they but dreamt of this, if they once guessed
us friends,
Where were our triumph then ?   A marriage, for
sane ends,
Is not a very tempting article, I fear,
To fine, fantastic—geese ! So, since they lived
not near,
We hid from them all plans that pointed Hymen's
way,
Till school and college sent them home to stay.
Then, I,—remembering that stolen love
Tastes sweet as stolen fruit,—and that above
All other joys they 'd prize a guilty bliss,—
I planned our deadly hatred. [*He chuckles.*] After
this—
And through *my* cunning—we, the warring sires,
Need only condescend to our desires.

PASQUIN.

But how confess it ? how conceal our arts ?
Cats let from bags would startle such young
                                                    hearts.
I dubbed you Ass—and Rogue,—a very Knave
                                                    indeed !

BERGAMIN.

Ass was sufficient.   Man should not exceed.

PASQUIN.

What pretext ?

BERGAMIN.

            There you are, old man !   Your girl
Herself suggested—[*corrects himself*]—gave, at
                                                    least, the twirl
To my Idea,—thus made doubly mine.
Here, and to-night, they planned to meet, in fine.
My youngster will be first.—Just as your girl he
                                                    sees,
Ruffians, in masks, shall start from out the trees.
They seize her :—she despairs : and lo ! young
                                                    Chanticleer
Darts to her rescue, without pause or fear.
The ruffians fly his flashing, conquering blade :—
They fly.—We show ourselves.—The rescued maid
Sobs in your arms.—You wipe a tear or so,
And bless her hero-saviour.—I relent.—Tableau !

PASQUIN
[*with enthusiasm*].
I call that genius.   Yes, by heaven I do!

BERGAMIN
[*modestly*].
Genius?   Ah well! old friend, *I* won't say no!
—But see, who comes— ?   Hush now.—Observe
                                                    him well.
That man approaching—that is Straforel,—
   [STRAFOREL *is seen in the magnificent costume of
      a Bravo, slowly and majestically advancing
      down stage.*]
The famous bravo, freelance, cavalier.
—I wrote to him but now—that's why he's here.—
'Tis *he* abducts your girl.
   [BERGAMIN *descends hastily from wall, and
         bows to* STRAFOREL.]

BERGAMIN.
                        Allow me, first of all,
Sir, to present my friend,——

STRAFOREL
[*bowing*].
                        Sir— ?
[*He looks about him, puzzled to see no one.*]

BERGAMIN
[*pointing to* PASQUIN, *a-straddle the wall*].
                        —Pasquin.   On the wall.

STRAFOREL
[*aside*].
Faith ! a new setting for an ancient fool !

BERGAMIN
[*pompous*].
My scheme, sir, would impress——

STRAFOREL
[*sardonic*].
　　　　　　—an infant school !

BERGAMIN
[*taken aback*].
—Man of experience.—Ha ! you act——

STRAFOREL
[*bowing*].
　　　　　—and hold my peace.

BERGAMIN.
Ha ! an abduction, then ; with fighting, if you
　　　　　　　　　　　　　please.

STRAFOREL.
That's understood.

BERGAMIN.
　　Ah ! but with prudent, careful men,
Who will not hurt my boy, [*pompous*] my Son

STRAFOREL.

Oh,—then,
I 'll take the foils myself,——

BERGAMIN.

Your humble servant, sir.
[*They bow.*]

PASQUIN
[*to* BERGAMIN].
You ask him what it costs.

BERGAMIN
[*embarrassed*].

Ahem! I hope I—er—.
For an abduction, now—what is the usual charge?

STRAFOREL
[*with a swagger*].
Sir, that depends. The price is small and
large:
It goes by merit. If I 've understood,
What *you* require is something neat and good.
I, in your place, should order—a first-class.
[*Bowing, with flourish.*]

BERGAMIN
[*dazzled*].
Is there such choice?

STRAFOREL.

I'd rather think there was!
Sir! we've the obvious, open, schoolboy rape,
Which only needs black cloaks, no matter what
their shape;
The rape by cab;—'tis little in request;—
The rape by day—the rape by night looks best;—
The pompous rape with coaches of the court,
With powdered lacqueys, wigs of every sort—
(The wigs are extra)—eunuchs, slaves, and mutes,
Blacks, bravos, brigands, musketeers—as suits;
The rape done with postillions, three or four,
And half a dozen horses, less or more;—
The decorous rape, in dowager's landau—
It is not popular, a trifle slow;—
The comic rape:—the lady must be fond;—
Romantic, in a boat;—requires a pond;—
The rape Venetian—wants a blue lagoon;—
The rape by moonlight, or without a moon—
Moonlight is dear, and always in demand;—
The rape lugubrious, by blue lightning planned,
With challenge, single combats, clash of arms,
Great flapping hats, dark cloaks, and war's
alarms;—
The rape emphatic, and the rape polite;—
The rape with torches, *that's* a charming sight!
The rape in masks—we call that classical;—
The rape gallant, done to sweet music's call;—
The rape in sedan chair, that's new and gay,
The latest thing of all—and *distingué.*

BERGAMIN

[*scratching his head, to* PASQUIN].
What do you think ?

PASQUIN.

And you ?

BERGAMIN.

I think that—dash the cost !
I think we should strike *hard*. Try *everything*—
almost !
Order a rape——

STRAFOREL.

With trimmings ? As you like.

BERGAMIN.

Imagination is the thing to strike.
Cloaks—sedan chairs—music—a torch—a mask !

STRAFOREL

[*taking notes in a book*].
I see, I see. I'll make it now my task
To group the articles. As extras. With first-
class.

BERGAMIN.

Good !

C

STRAFOREL.

Soon I shall return. But, that my men
may pass,
This gentleman's park gate [*looking at* PASQUIN]
must stand ajar.

BERGAMIN.

It shall be opened.

STRAFOREL.

My lords, [*bows with flourish*] au revoir !
[*Stopping before going off.*]
A first-class, and with extras.   That 's the plan !
[*Exit, swaggering.*]

PASQUIN.

With all his show of honesty, your man
Has never named his price.

BERGAMIN.

Oh, let that trifle go !
Think ! we shall share one hearth ; this wall shall
be laid low.

PASQUIN.

Sweet thought ! next winter but one rent to pay !

BERGAMIN.

We 'll study to improve these gardens, day by
day.

PASQUIN.

We'll trim the oldest trees.

BERGAMIN.

We'll pave the woodland ways.

PASQUIN.

Our monograms, in brightest flowers, shall blaze
United, in one frame.

BERGAMIN.

Where gloomy oak-trees grow——

PASQUIN

[*interrupting*].

—we'll light 'em up a bit.   Hang glass balls in
a row!

BERGAMIN.

We'll make a brand-new pond, for goldfish to
adorn.

PASQUIN.

We'll have a fountain too; a rockery of our own;
A rockery set with ferns—with *ferns*, old chap,
you hear?

BERGAMIN.

What can man ask for more?

PASQUIN.

We'll bask in bliss, that's clear.

BERGAMIN.

You've married off your girl.

PASQUIN.

You've given your lad employ.

BERGAMIN.

Ah, my dear Pasquin!

PASQUIN.

Ah, my dear old boy!

[*They fall into one another's arms.* PERCINET *and* SYLVETTE *enter abruptly from different sides.*]

SYLVETTE

[*seeing her father clasp* BERGAMIN, *and thinking they are fighting*].

Ah!

BERGAMIN

[*seeing* SYLVETTE, *to* PASQUIN].

Lord!   Your daughter!

PERCINET

[*seeing his father grasping* PASQUIN].

Ah!

PASQUIN

[*to* BERGAMIN, *seeing* PERCINET].

The boy !

BERGAMIN

[*aside to* PASQUIN].

Let 's fight !

[*They turn their embrace into a wrestling match.*]

PASQUIN.

Ruffian !

BERGAMIN.

You villain !

SYLVETTE

[*catching her father by his coat-tails*].

Papa !

PERCINET -

[*same business with* BERGAMIN].

Papa !

PASQUIN.

Right !

I 'll teach you to insult me——

BERGAMIN.

You struck first——

PASQUIN.

Liar !

SYLVETTE.

Papa——

BERGAMIN.

Thief !

PERCINET.

Father——

PASQUIN.

Brigand !

BERGAMIN.

Thrice accursed !

SYLVETTE.

Papa——

[*They succeed in separating them.*]

PERCINET

[*dragging off his father*].

Come home.   'Tis late.

BERGAMIN

[*struggling*].

I 'll tear his vitals out !

[PERCINET *leads him off.*]

PASQUIN

[*same business with* SYLVETTE].

I foam with rage !

SYLVETTE

[*leading him off*].
'Tis damp.   Think if you caught the gout !

[*The daylight begins to fade slowly.   The stage remains empty a moment.   Then, in* PAS-QUIN'S *park, L., enter* STRAFOREL, *his* MASKS, MUSICIANS, BRAVOS, *etc.*]

STRAFOREL

[*with an air*].

Already the blue sky assumes a star.—
[*In a different voice, placing his men, pushing them about, etc.*]

Stand there,—and there.—And you—.   Stay as
you are.
—Soon we shall hear the pensive vesper-bell,
See gentle Sylvia, all in white, appear.—
I give the signal.—

[*Looking up, he sees the moon rising.*]

Damme ! that looks well !
Here comes the moon.—Booked for success, that's
clear.

[*He examines the extravagant cloaks of the*
BRAVOS.]

Excellent cloaks.—But let the rapiers show.
Clap hand to hilt. [*To the nearest* BRAVO.] Truss
me those coat-tails. So !

[*The sedan chair is brought by* BLACK BEARERS.]

That chair comes over here. [*Looking at* BEARERS.]
Those blacks ?—Not bad at all.—

[*Speaking off stage.*]

Torch-bearers, over there— ! don't move until I
call.

[*The back of the stage is lighted with vague rosy
reflections from the torches behind the trees.
Enter the* MUSICIANS.]

The players ? Let them group where the lights
shine like roses.

[*He arranges them at the back.*]

—Gracefully, now, and free.—Don't all take the
same poses !
Stand up, you mandoline.—Sit down there, you.
—Kneel ; so—
There ! [*fatuously*] that's *my* concert,—worthy
of Watteau.

[*Severely to a* BRAVO.]
Number One mask! what ails those trembling
knees?
Attention, sir! With spirit!—Now then, please;
Tune up, musicians.—Softly with that tune!—
Soft,—soft,—and thrilling.—So.—And none too
soon.
[*He masks.*]

[PERCINET *enters slowly, right of wall. While he
is speaking the night falls, and stars appear.*]

PERCINET.

My father looks appeased, and I have fled.
This floating breath of elder-blossom seems
To mingle with my brain. The day is dead,
[*he looks about him*]
The lovely day.—The flowers fade to dreams.

STRAFOREL
[*aside*].

Music!

PERCINET.

I feel—I tremble like a leaf.—
What ails me? *She* is coming—.

STRAFOREL
[*to* MUSICIANS].

Lower that stress!

PERCINET.

She comes—to Me!—O Sweetheart, past belief
I love you!—And the wind sounds like your
dress.
The flowers fade—or are my eyes grown dim?
The flowers fade, yet still their sweetness grows.

[*He looks up.*]

Yon star seems hanging down from Heaven's
rim.
And who makes music?—See! the darkness
grows.—

Yes, the sweet night has come; and now
About the heaven's darkened brow
I see the stars, in shining row,
        Light one by one.
The ponds awake, and, croaking, hail the dark;
The stars redouble, spark by fiery spark;
The moon—a swinging, growing, crescent bark—
        Is pale and wan.

Diamonds and sapphires—jewels of the skies!—
I was your lover once; and otherwise
I sang your praises, ere I saw Her rise
        Veiled all in white.
But I have fairer matter for my lays
Since that my Sylvia, with her childish ways
And soft hair clipped, child-fashion, round her face,
        Brought the New Light.

Familiar stars ! my stars in heaven shining,
Whose numbers far exceed my poor divining,
Your beauty will indeed be reft and pining
    When, through the twilight's bars,
She shall appear above the garden's vapours.
—Seeing Her eyes, your ineffective tapers
Shall pale, and cease their self-condemnèd labours—
    Poor, jealous stars !

[*A bell rings, far off.   Enter* SYLVETTE, *L.*]

SYLVETTE.

The vesper-bell.   He waits—

[*A shrill signal-whistle.*   STRAFOREL *starts up
before her ; the torches appear.*]

Ah !

[*The* BRAVOS *seize her and thrust her rapidly
into the sedan chair.*]

Rescue here !

PERCINET

[*starting forward*].

Damnation !

SYLVETTE.

Percinet !

PERCINET.

I 'm coming, dear !

[*He draws sword, leaps over the wall, and fights
with several of the* BRAVOS.]

Hold—Hold—Hold—

[*Fighting.*]

STRAFOREL

[*to the* MUSICIANS].

Tremolo !

[*The* FIDDLES *execute a dramatic tremolo.*   *The*
BRAVOS *fly and disperse.*]

[*With theatrical emphasis.*]

Now, by great Zeus,
The boy 's a hero !

[*Duel between* PERCINET *and* STRAFOREL.   STRA-
FOREL *suddenly claps his hand to his heart,
drops his sword, and staggers back.*]

Help ! Help !
[*Groans.*]

'Tis no use—.

[*He falls.*]

PERCINET

[*running to* SYLVETTE].

Sylvia!

[*Tableau. She is in the sedan chair, he on his knees before her.*]

SYLVETTE.

My hero!

PASQUIN

[*appearing suddenly*].

Son of Bergamin!

[*To* SYLVETTE.]

What! Your preserver?—Girl! you shall wed him!

Son!—Hero!

PERCINET AND SYLVETTE.

Heavens!

[BERGAMIN *has entered on his own side, followed by* SERVANTS *bearing torches.*]

PASQUIN

[*to* BERGAMIN, *who appears on the crest of the wall*].

O Bergamin, forgive!

BERGAMIN

[*solemnly*].

My hate is shattered.

PASQUIN.

Let the children live !

PERCINET.

Sylvia, we 're dreaming.   Sylvia, do not seem
To breathe too deeply, lest we break our dream

BERGAMIN.

Feuds end in marriage since the first play writ.
—I am for peace.   [*Pointing to the wall.*]   Let us
have done with it !

PERCINET.

Who would have thought my father thus could
bend ?

SYLVETTE

[*simply*].

I always knew there 'd be a happy end.

[*As they retire up stage with* PASQUIN, STRA-
FOREL *rises on his arm and holds out paper
on the point of his sword to* BERGAMIN.]

BERGAMIN.

Hullo !   What 's that ?   A paper ?   [*He takes it.*]
Wait until
I 've seen the signature.   *What 's this ?*

STRAFOREL

[*bowing*].

My little bill !

[*He falls back.*]

CURTAIN.

END OF ACT I.

ACT II

SCENE—*Same as in* ACT I., *but the wall has disappeared. The stone benches which were against it have been moved R. and L. Modifications in the details: flower-beds, clumps of pampas-grass, trellised arbours, pretentious statues of imitation marble, greenhouse. R. a garden table ; chairs.*

The curtain rises on PASQUIN *seated on bench L. reading a newspaper. At the back of the stage* BLAISE *with a rake.*

BLAISE

[raking].

They tells me, master, Lawyer comes to-
night? . . .
Heigh ! [*leans on rake*] 'tis a month since that
old wall went flat,
And you've kept house together.—Well, that's
right !

[*Goes on raking, then stops to chuckle.*]
Our pretty lovers won't complain o' *that* !

PASQUIN

[*raising his head and looking about him*].

Looks well without the wall, eh ?

BLAISE.

Lovely, sir.

PASQUIN

[*complacently*].

Yes ; an improvement. Cent. per cent., and—
[*He bends over and feels a tuft of grass.*] Hey ?—
Who's wet *my* grass ? [*Furious.*] Some donkey,
I infer,
Has brought an early watering-pot this way.
[*With explosion.*] Water *at night*, old ob-
stinate !

BLAISE

[*calmly.*]

'Twas he—
'Twas Master Bergamin, sir ; never me.

PASQUIN.

Bergamin ? Hah ! [*With an effort.*] Well, well—.
He will hold fast
To his own fancy.—' Water, first and last.'

D

As if judicious sprinkling, done with tact and
care ; . . .
Well, well !

[*To* BLAISE.]

—Bring out those flowering plants from there.

[BLAISE *sets in a row a lot of plants he fetches
from the greenhouse.* PASQUIN *reads his
paper.* BERGAMIN *appears at the back
carrying an enormous water-pot.*]

BERGAMIN

[*watering the shrubs abundantly*].

Hah !   Stinted.   Stinted of their natural food.—
Plants require *oceans* to do any good.—

[*Speaking to a tree.*]

Thirsty, old boy ?—I dearly love a tree !
—There ! [*watering*] take a bucketful, and think
o' me !
Another ?—Hah ! [*watering*] my park looks trim
and neat.
Nice, decent statues.

[*Puts down watering-pot and addresses tree.*]

There ! you 've had your treat.

[*Catching sight of* PASQUIN.]

'Ullo !

Good morning.

[*No answer.*]

'Morning.

[*No answer. With indignation.*]

I said,—'morning, sir !

PASQUIN

[*looking up, wearily*].

I see you all day long.—Oh, dear.—Why make
this stir ?

BERGAMIN

[*taken aback*].

Hey ?—Well ?

[*He sees* BLAISE *arranging the pots. Roars.*]

Take in that stuff !

[BLAISE, *alarmed, drags off the plants hurriedly.*
PASQUIN *lifts his eyes to heaven, shrugs his
shoulders, and reads.* BERGAMIN *strolls up
and down, looking bored and unoccupied. He
ends by sitting down beside* PASQUIN. *Silence.
He speaks with a melancholy air.*]

Once, on a happier day,
This was the hour I chose to hide and steal away.

PASQUIN

[*dreamily, lowering his paper*].

I used to creep from home on light and thief-like
toe.

Ah ! [*he sighs*] *then* I was amused !

BERGAMIN.

Our secret— ?

PASQUIN
[*sighing*].

Yes; I know.

BERGAMIN.

Those children to mislead—to lure from off our
track;
Plots, plans, intrigues to build ere we could get
our crack——

PASQUIN.

To daily risk one's life.   To daily climb that
wall—
Careless of collar-bones, and ribs, and dare the
fall!

BERGAMIN.

My conversation—your soliloquies—
Paid for by ruses such as Indians prize—.

PASQUIN.

Through furzy bushes forced to pick one's way,—
Yes, *that* amused me!

BERGAMIN.

On all fours, one day,
I crept triumphant—greened my breeches too!

PASQUIN

[*regretfully*].

We always, for abuse, found something new.

BERGAMIN.

Always some new charge.

PASQUIN.

Ah, that *was* amusing !
[*He yawns.*]

Old man ?

BERGAMIN

[*yawning*].

Yes, Pasquin.

PASQUIN

[*mysteriously*].

We miss that abusing.

BERGAMIN

[*quickly*].

What stuff !

[*After reflecting.*]

We're dull—

Well, ye—es. It's true.

And *this* is
The Vengeance of Romance !

[*A silence.　He watches* PASQUIN, *who goes
on reading.　Aside.*]

　　　　　　　　　　—His waistcoat misses
Its daily button.　Oh, dear me !

[*He gets up, walks away, returns, moves uneasily.*]

PASQUIN

[*looking at him over the top of his paper, aside*].

　　　　　　　　　　　　Poor wretch !
Poor, huge cockchafer ! ever on the stretch.

[*He pretends to read as* BERGAMIN *passes him
again.*]

BERGAMIN

[*watching him, aside*].

Yes.　When he reads, he squints.

[*Goes up stage, whistling.*]

PASQUIN

[*aside, irritably*].

　　　　　　He whistles—it's a trick !
That everlasting tune !　[*Aloud.*]　Dear boy, it
　　　　　　　　　　　makes me sick.

BERGAMIN

[*smiling sardonically*].

My dear old chap! [*with a superior air*] it is not
                                        hard to spy
The mote that lurks within a neighbour's eye.
But your own beams——

PASQUIN.

Mine ? Mine ?

BERGAMIN

[*with irritation*].

        Can't you stand still ?   O dear !
I don't deny your cold ; your head is none so
                                        clear ;
But need you *always* sniff ?—sniff comes from
                                        snuff—
And twenty times a day——

PASQUIN
[*interrupting*]
                There, there !   *E*nough !

BERGAMIN.

And *forty* times a day you tell the same old story !
—At dinner, your bread-pills keep up their
                                trajectory.—

[PASQUIN, *listening to him, seated, swings his foot
        to and fro impatiently.*]

You cannot even sit in your own elbow-
                                        chair
Unless you shake a leg.   [*Critically.*]   They 're
                            not a handsome pair !

PASQUIN.

All right.   Now we are grown blue-mouldy with
                                        ennui,
You 've nothing better left than to pick holes
                                        in me.—
You 've counted up *my* faults—made a damn
                                        friendly list ;
But life in common, sir, homelife 's an oculist !
—*My* cataract 's removed, I 'd have you know.—
                                        I see
How false you are ! how base ! a miser ;—worse
                                        than me !
You 're like a fly to microscopic view !—
Your faults all swell, and swell—.
            [*Holds up hands of horror.*]
                            The monstrous crew !
            [*A short silence.*]

BERGAMIN

[*with affected indifference*].

What I once questioned, I don't doubt at
                                        all.

PASQUIN

[*naïvely*].

What ?

BERGAMIN

[*pointing to where wall stood*].
You miss *that*.

PASQUIN.
You 're *lost* without the wall !

BERGAMIN.
Thanks.   I 've enough of seeing you each day.

PASQUIN

[*violently*].
My life is gone, since you came here to stay.

BERGAMIN

[*very dignified*].
Well, sir, 'tis well.   'Tis very good indeed.
Our plans were laid, I think——

PASQUIN.
To suit another's need !

BERGAMIN.
For our poor children's sake——

PASQUIN.
—It was of them I spoke.—
[*Convinced, with emotion.*]
Yes.   Let us bend our heads, in silence, 'neath
that yoke.
—O my lost freedom !

BERGAMIN
[*bitterly*].
Parents *always* pay.
—They *live* by sacrifice.—
[SYLVETTE *and* PERCINET *appear L., back of
stage, among the trees ; they slowly cross the
stage, clasping one another, and with exalted
gestures.*]

PASQUIN
[*to* BERGAMIN].
Hush ! hush, I say !
—*E*nter the Lovers.

BERGAMIN
[*sneering*].
Hah ! the newest pose is
To walk about in your apotheosis.

PASQUIN.
Since the betrothal they 're absurd, I swear !—
[*discontentedly*]
You 'd think that they wore haloes in their hair.

BERGAMIN.

This is the hour when—mimicking the slow
And pious gestures of Love's Pilgrim's Show—
They come each day ; and here, as at a shrine,
Adore the sacred scene—of Straforel's rapine.

[SYLVETTE *and* PERCINET, *who disappeared from right, reappear and come slowly down stage.*]

BERGAMIN.

Lo ! the Young Pilgrims !

PASQUIN.

Worshipping themselves !
—Let's hide and listen.

[*They retire behind a clump of shrubs, and are seen at intervals listening, peering over the bushes, etc.*]

PERCINET.

—how above all else
I love you—.

SYLVETTE

[*in a murmur*].

—love you—. [*They pause.*]
Hallowed spot, and dear— !

[*She points to the place of the rape.*]

PERCINET.

Yes, here it happened; [*pointing*] that last brute
fell here.

SYLVETTE.

I was Andromeda, chained to yon rock:

PERCINET.

Here, I was Perseus.

SYLVETTE.

Love !—the sudden shock—.
I could not count your foes.   You fought
with——

PERCINET.

Perhaps ten.

SYLVETTE.

Ten ?   They were twenty ! all gigantic men.
—And that last ravening monster whom you
slew !
Thirty [*with conviction*]—at least !

PERCINET

[*modestly*].

Thirty ;—or thirty-two.

SYLVETTE

[*adoring him*].

Tell me once more how, with his sword in hand,
And eyes ablaze, My Conqueror drove that band.

PERCINET.

I first engaged in tierce—[*hesitating*]—at least,
I think—.
[*Fatuously.*]
I only know they fell, and fell, as pebbles sink.

SYLVETTE.

Dear, if it were not for your golden hair
You would be Cæsar !

PERCINET.

Yes, [*deprecating*] *I am*—more fair.

SYLVETTE

[*with enthusiasm*].

What lacks our love but to be writ in song ?

PERCINET.

Darling, it shall be.

SYLVETTE.

Darling !

PERCINET.

We'll prolong
Our love through epics.

SYLVETTE.

O, how dreams come true!
For you must know,—long ere I met with you—
I vowed to wed some high heroic mate—
Some one my father would think—desperate!

PERCINET.

Sweet!

SYLVETTE

[*confidentially*].

O, *his* choice was—just the Usual Man,
The blameless creature girls refuse,—who can!
Though, still encouraged by his maiden aunts,
The object '*dares to hope.*' [*Scornfully.*] *He* 'dares'!

PERCINET.

Or vaunts
His father's riches:—says, 'His father's trees
March with *your* father's orchard.' [*With an
outburst.*] Families!
What crimes are still committed in your name!
Romance how wronged! High love how bowed
and tame!

BERGAMIN

[*behind his tree*].

Pooh !

SYLVETTE

[*clasping her hands*].

O how true !—But, Percinet, [*laughing*]
how cross
Our fathers have become ! They—snarl——

PERCINET

[*laughing*].

They gore and toss !
They paw the earth !

PASQUIN

[*protesting*].

Ahem !

PERCINET

[*lightly, scornfully*].

I know the reason why.

BERGAMIN

[*curiously*].

Hallo— ? [*Peers over bush.*]

PERCINET.

Crawling on earth, they have to watch
                                    us fly !
—How should their ashes understand our flame ?

BERGAMIN.

Young devil !   [*Looking over bush.*]

PERCINET.

I *respect* them all the same—
Good, worthy burghers : only, are they quite——

PASQUIN

[*indignantly*].

Quite what ?

PERCINET.

To call them—jealous—would not be polite.

SYLVETTE

[*cheerfully*].

Of course, *they* only fill a second place.

PERCINET

[*laughing*].

My beaver's cocked too high to suit *their* ways.

SYLVETTE.

Your father, in your presence, has the air,
The awkward air of—[*coquettishly*]—dare I say it ?

PERCINET.

Dare !

SYLVETTE.

A tame duck who has hatched an eagle's egg.

BERGAMIN
[*aside*].

God bless my soul !

SYLVETTE
[*laughing still more exasperatingly*].

Their pardon I could beg——

PASQUIN
[*aside*].

Quite right !

SYLVETTE.

—when I remember how we fooled them, dear ;
We, helped by Love.

PERCINET.

Oh ! Destiny is clear
Upon that point.   However loves meander,
Kind Fate still plays the valet to Leander.

E

BERGAMIN

[*scornfully*].

Ho! ho!

SYLVETTE

[*sentimental; after a short pause*].

Our marriage-contract hour draws near.

PERCINET.

Oh! I forgot the fiddles!

SYLVETTE

[*reproachfully*].

Oh, my dear!

PERCINET

[*apologetic*].

I fly!

SYLVETTE

[*tenderly*].

Nay, I forgive.

[*She stops him as he starts off.*]

Your lady condescends
To walk with you to where the greensward ends.

[*They walk off together, embracing one another.*
SYLVETTE *bridles, and speaks with many airs
and graces.*]

SYLVETTE.

The great Old Lovers were, methinks, like Us.

PERCINET.

Yes; we take rank in the Immortal Band.

SYLVETTE.

Romeo and Juliet,——

PERCINET.

Thisbe; Pyramus,——

SYLVETTE.

Arminta and her Shepherd,——

PERCINET.

Iseult, the White Hand.

SYLVETTE.

And Guinevere,——

[*They go off the scene, but their voices are still heard behind the trees.*]

The voice of PERCINET.

He, of the Naked Sword,——

The voice of SYLVETTE.

Petrarch and Laura,——

[*The voices die away.*]

BERGAMIN

[*coming out from behind the shrubbery*].

O good Lord !   Go-od Lord !

PASQUIN

[*following him and speaking with derision*].

My compliments, dear sir, upon your plan,

[*bows derisively*]

Your great success, O great, sagacious man !
No doubt it serves some secret end you had,
But, in one word, you 've driven those children
                                        —mad !

BERGAMIN.

Well, yes, your girl is certainly a bore.
She and her rape !   [*Shrugs his shoulders.*]   Was
                    no maid wed before ?

PASQUIN

[*piqued*].

As for your son, the Hero-Popinjay, [*irritably*]
My nerves won't stand his airs another day.

BERGAMIN.

But what revolts *me* is the way they dare
Discuss us both—as if we only were
Two harmless idiots of inferior sort.
We shut our eyes and let them have their sport,
And when we shut our eyes they call us—blind.
[*Pettishly.*]
I am a fool for minding, yet I mind !

PASQUIN

[*same manner*].

Had you not thought of that, sagacious man ?
Was that no part of your inspirèd plan ?
—Ho ! here's a youth who sets us in our true
place,
And as for *him*—the king may tie his shoe-lace !

BERGAMIN.

I 'll lace him yet !

PASQUIN.

I 'm going to tell them—all.

BERGAMIN.

No, no ! Not yet ! Don't be nonsensical !
—Wait for the marriage. [*Grimly.*] As a
wedding gift
We 'll tell 'em some few facts. Till then, make
shift
To look as dumb as—fish.

PASQUIN.

Fish caught in their own net.
—But that's your plan, no doubt—your plan !
[*Shrugging his shoulders.*]

BERGAMIN

[*angrily*].

Sir ! you forget,
You egged me on.

PASQUIN.

I ?—Never !   'Twas mere fun.

BERGAMIN

[*aside*].

This man will drive me mad !
[*Enter* SYLVETTE *gaily.   She has a branch of blossom in her hand, with which she makes signs off stage to* PERCINET, *whom she has just left.   She comes down stage, smiling, and stands between the two fathers.*]

SYLVETTE

[*gaily*].

Good morning, every one.
Good morning, my papa !—Father-in-law, good
day !

BERGAMIN

[*sulkily*].

'Day, future daughter.

SYLVETTE

[*imitating his voice*].

Fu—ture daugh—ter !

What a way !   [*Pertly.*]

—You look *so* cross.

BERGAMIN

[*sulkily*].

It's Pasquin——

[SYLVETTE, *shaking the branch to and fro before
his face, and speaking patronisingly as to a
naughty child.*]

SYLVETTE.

Hu—sh !   Be calm !
I come as Peace.   Behold me with my Palm !

[*She waves branch affectedly.   Patronisingly.*]

You hate each other still a little, eh ?

[*She looks from one to the other.*]

—Rome was not built, remember, in one day.—
And you were foes so long——

PASQUIN

[*aside*].

O irony of Fáte!

BERGAMIN

[i*ronical*].

Most true, most wise young maid! You're
witness to our hate.

SYLVETTE.

A mortal hatred, too!—Oh, I remember well
The things *you* used to say—.
[*Pointing to* BERGAMIN *with her branch.*]
Don't fear! [*coquettishly*] I
shall not tell
All that you said of *him*—
[*pointing to* PASQUIN]
—there, by your big rose-bed,
And never guessed, ha, ha! that I heard all you
said,
Hid by my dear old wall.

BERGAMIN

[*aside*].

The girl's a simple fool!

SYLVETTE

[*turning to* PASQUIN].

For [*with emphasis*] every single day,—at dawn,
—by twilight cool,—
I met my Percinet! And neither of you
once
—No, neither!—had a doubt.

PASQUIN

[*ironically*].

Forgive me, I'm a dunce :
And *he*—— [*pointing to* BERGAMIN].

SYLVETTE

[*with importance, interrupting*].

For you must know, I saw him *every day.*

[*To* BERGAMIN.]

—Do you remember still that time my Percinet
Swore he would wed romance ? Ha, ha! How
wild you were !
I heard it all. And you'll admit, dear sir,
Percinet keeps his word.

BERGAMIN

[*vexed*].

You think so ? [*Sneering.*] You're quite sure ?
And if I laid my plans——

SYLVETTE

[*Pompously, imitating* PERCINET'S *way of speaking*].
Plans change. Lovers endure.
[*Childishly.*]
I've read, a hundred times, how lovers' dreams
succeed
And cruel fathers yield. Why should they not,
indeed ?
They 're human, after all. They can't *want* to be
hated.

BERGAMIN.

They can't— ? O let me laugh !
[*To* SYLVETTE, *ironically.*]
—So *that's* how you got mated ?

SYLVETTE

[*tossing her head*].
We 've proved it true !

BERGAMIN.

Oh, if I cared to say——

SYLVETTE

[*quickly*].
What ?

BERGAMIN.

Nothing!

SYLVETTE
[*after looking at him; with discomfort*].
You look—very strange to-day.

BERGAMIN
[*ironically*].
Why should I? [*Aside.*] Ho! I almost think
I will——

PASQUIN.

With just one word—.
[*Aside, going up stage.*]
Best keep the secret still.
[*A slight pause.*]

SYLVETTE
[*defiantly, but uneasily*].
'Tis easiest not to speak when naught's to say!

PASQUIN
[*turning about, in an explosive manner*].
Naught? Naught, she calls it? Poor tricked,
blinded may!
What! [*turning on her*] you believe that things
can happen *so*?
That locked park gates fly open at a blow?

BERGAMIN

[*same manner*].

She thinks, ho ! ho ! that Love still wears a mask !

SYLVETTE

[*puzzled, offended, half suspicious*].

I—I believe—.   What do you mean ?

BERGAMIN

[*getting excited*].

I ask
Yourself, what do *you* mean ? Since this old world
began,
Poets, and love-sick fools, exalt the *younger* man—
Poets, and idiot girls, who make their boast
That only curling locks shall rule the roast.
But lo ! the hour of vengeance now has struck,
And wigs—your *fathers'* wigs—have all the luck.

SYLVETTE.

But——

BERGAMIN

[*growing excited*].

Oh, I know !   I know we represent
All that is out of date, and weak, and impotent !
[*Mocking.*]
Poor doting men who doze in thick night-gear ;
Dull cats while mice carouse.—We 've heard *you*
talking, dear !

But those are ancient tales.   The modern father,
                                                         Miss,
You 'll find—I fear you 'll find—is very far from
                                                          this.
And   as   we   knew   you   both — you   and   your
                                                        Percinet—
We just forbade your love, to *make you* disobey!

SYLVETTE.

What!   [*Overcome.*]   What!—you *knew?*

PASQUIN
[*triumphant*].
        Of course we did, you—child!

SYLVETTE
[*still incredulous*].
Our meetings— ?

BERGAMIN
[*patronising*].
I applauded!

PASQUIN.
                   And *I* smiled!

SYLVETTE.
The—benches that we climbed— ?

PASQUIN.

I placed them there for you.

SYLVETTE.

The—duel ?

BERGAMIN

[*bows mockingly*].

Our small joke !

SYLVETTE.

The bravos ?

PASQUIN

[*bows same way*].

Our paid crew !

SYLVETTE.

My rape ? [*With sudden fire.*]   Ah no !—'Tis false !

BERGAMIN

[*searching in his pockets*].

I 'll show you,—that I will !

—Here, in my pocket, see——

[*He produces* STRAFOREL'S *bill.* SYLVETTE *snatches
the paper from him and tears it open.*]

SYLVETTE

[*reading aloud*].

   'To Straforel (as per bill) :
One imitation rape, to bring betrothal on—'
Ah ! [*She reads.*] '*E*ight best bravos' cloaks,
   with discount, two pounds one.
*E*ight masks——'

BERGAMIN

[*to* PASQUIN, *uneasily, after watching her*].

  Upon my life ! I think we spoke too soon.

SYLVETTE

[*reading*].

'One sedan chair, silk lined——'
[*She looks up.*] It *was* silk ! [*Reads.*] 'One full
         moon.'
[*Ironically.*] I see you spared no pains !
  [*She throws down the bill on the table and
   laughs nervously.*]

PASQUIN

[*surprised*].

  Then you 're not angry, dear ?

SYLVETTE

[*with elaborate graciousness*].

Papa ! 'tis all a joke.

[*Turning sweetly to* BERGAMIN.]

You've wasted wit, I fear,
Dear Master Bergamin, if you indeed suppose
I only love your son for reasons such as—those.
[*She points to paper on table.*]

PASQUIN

[*delighted*].

She takes it very well!

BERGAMIN

[*to* SYLVETTE].

You take it very well!

PASQUIN.

Shall *I* tell Percinet?

SYLVETTE

[*sharply*].

For Heaven's sake, don't tell!
[*Recovering herself, and smiling, with an effort.*]
—Don't tell him. Men, you know, dear father,
                        are so—curious

BERGAMIN

[*approving*].

Now, here's good sense at last.

[*To* SYLVETTE.]

I thought you would be furious,
But [*looking at his watch*] oh, by Jove, it's time—!
—It's time to go and dress.
Your contract's still to sign.
[H*olding out his hand to* SYLVETTE.]
—Good friends?

SYLVETTE

[*with honeyed smiles*].

I can't express
How much I thank you, sir!
[*She curtsies.*]

BERGAMIN

[*still a little doubtful, comes back*].

Then—you won't hate me, then?

SYLVETTE.

I?
[*He leaves the stage, followed by* PASQUIN. *She
looks after* BERGAMIN, *her whole expression
changing. She speaks with cold, deliberate
rage.*]
But I—think—you—are—the Very Worst
of men!

F

[*Enter* PERCINET *joyously.*]

PERCINET

Still where I left you, darling?   Can't you bear
                                                to go
Far from the memoried spot which saw me strike
                                            that blow?
A rare adventure!   [*Joyously.*]   Love! you prize
                                                it well.

SYLVETTE
[*stonily*].

I—prize it.

PERCINET.

        There!—just by your foot, you fell
Half-fainting, yet alive, to watch me slay a host—
Thirty strong men!

SYLVETTE

[*pettishly.*]
Say—*ten.*   And at the very most.

PERCINET

[*solicitously, drawing nearer*].
Darling, what ails you?   You look sad, most dear!
Surely [*fatuously*] those mem'ries do not still
                                            cause fear?
—O blue eyes! smile from out those gathering
                                                mists!
Blue sapphire eyes, that melt to amethysts!

SYLVETTE

[*aside*].

I call that—stilted !

PERCINET

[*reassuringly*].

Oh, I see—I guess !
What tender sadness lurks about this place.
—You miss our dear, our sacred moss-grown wall,
Which sheltered our young hopes and our sweet
fears ;
Yet what is glory-crowned can never truly
fall,—
Our Romeo's balcony survives the stress of years.

SYLVETTE

[*impatient, irritated*].

Ah !

PERCINET

[*lyrically*].

In the splendour of eternal morn,
Bathed in young light, that white old balcony
Still bears a silken ladder, all unworn,
That flutters by an ever-blossoming tree.

[*She looks up impatiently, without speaking.*]

PERCINET

[*with increasing emphasis*].

—Unchanging background to undying passion !

SYLVETTE

[*irritated*].

Oh !

PERCINET.

That is how our own wall still is set,
Where, in the same romantic, magic fashion
We learned to love——

SYLVETTE

[*aside*].

What ! is he talking yet ?

PERCINET

[*with a fatuous smile*].

Lo, now, my lady in her sovereignty
Has deigned to order that our loves shall be
Proclaimed in fairest verse——

SYLVETTE

[*anxiously*].

And so ?

PERCINET

[*with beaming satisfaction*].

I have begun to write!

SYLVETTE

[*contemptuously*].

What! *you* make rhymes?

PERCINET

[*on his dignity*].

Love,—had I learned to fight?

[*Confidentially.*]

Hear my beginning. Just a lyric burst.

[*Recites.*]

The Father's Feud : A Poem.

SYLVETTE.

Oh!

PERCINET.

Book first.

[*He strikes an attitude for declaiming.*]

SYLVETTE.

Oh!

PERCINET.

What's the matter?

SYLVETTE.

Joy . . . pride . . . rapture . . . my nerves, dear !
[*She bursts into tears.*]
Oh, let me be alone !
[*She turns her back upon him, still sitting on the bench, and hides her face in her handkerchief.*]

PERCINET

[*bewildered*].

My Sweet ! I 'll leave you here.
[*Aside, with a meaning smile.*]
A day like this !—Poor little thing.—She 's shy.
[*He goes up stage R., sees on the table the paper containing* STRAFOREL'S *bill, and taking a pencil from his pocket sits down saying :*]
—We 'll note those lines, since inspirations fly.—
[*He begins to write, but stops, holding his pencil in the air, and reads.*]
'To Straforel is debtor : insomuch as he
'Did feign to die and fall, with all solemnity,
'Before a boy's weak blade : one torn coat, three
                                        pound ten ;
'—To wounded pride, ten guineas.'—
[*He smiles.*]
                            What strange men !
[*He continues reading to himself. The smile vanishes. His eyes become fixed and staring.*]

SYLVETTE

[*still on the bench, wiping her eyes*].

Oh, if he guessed, how his poor pride would bleed!
I almost said it once. I must take better heed.

PERCINET

[*getting up*].

Ho! ho!

[*He laughs with forced mirth.*]

SYLVETTE

[*turning towards him*].

What's that?

PERCINET

[*hiding the bill behind him*].

Oh, nothing!

SYLVETTE

[*aside*].

Ah, what care!

[*She sighs.*]

PERCINET

[*aside*].

I see now why they found no dead man there.

SYLVETTE

[*aside, rising*].

He seems abashed.   What would be best to
say ?

[*She moves towards him.   Seeing he does not
notice her, she says coquettishly :*]
You 've never said you like my gown to-day ?

PERCINET

[*absently*].

Blue does not suit you.   You should dress in pink.

SYLVETTE

[*aside, much alarmed*].

Blue—does—not—suit ?—He has begun to think!
[*Looking at the table.*]
I left that man's bill there !

PERCINET

[*irritably*].

What are you fussing over ?

SYLVETTE.

Nothing.   [*Aside.*]   Perhaps the wind has played
the thieving lover.
[*Aloud, shaking out her skirts.*]

Nothing.   I only looked at my despisèd dress.
It's—blue.   [*Aside.*]   If he has seen it he will
soon confess.
[*Aloud.*]   But where's your dear love-poem ?
[PERCINET *starts.   She takes his arm and
speaks coaxingly.*]
My dearest ! say it now !

PERCINET
[*sharply*].

Oh 'no !

SYLVETTE.
Yes.   Say it !

PERCINET.
No !

SYLVETTE
[*ironically*].
Not to redeem your vow ?

PERCINET.
My verses are not worth——

SYLVETTE
[*interrupting*].
Their cost we cannot tell !

PERCINET.

What do you mean ?
[*He starts, and looks at her, suspicious.*]

SYLVETTE.

I mean, [*violently*] they 're not
by Straforel !

PERCINET.

Why ! then she knows ?

SYLVETTE.

He knows ?

SYLVETTE AND PERCINET
[*together*].

I know ;—and so do you !
[*A silence.   They look at one another, then
laugh a forced laugh.*]

Ha ! ha ! ha !

PERCINET.

What a joke !

SYLVETTE.

Yes.   *What* a joke !   So—new.

PERCINET.

They 've made us play a part.

SYLVETTE

[*bitterly*].

And *such* a part, my dear!

PERCINET.

Our fathers were fast friends.

SYLVETTE.

Dear neighbours : yes, that's clear.

PERCINET.

Like brothers !

SYLVETTE.

Yes ; you seem—a cousin, if you please.
[*She drops an ironical curtsy.*]

PERCINET.

I wed—my cousin.

SYLVETTE

[*protesting*].

Oh !

PERCINET.

[*patronisingly.*]

'Tis—classic.

SYLVETTE.

Yet one sees
Marriages that are more———
[*She shrugs her shoulders slightly.*]
———Well! there's a certain beauty
When people can—like us—indulge in love, *and*
duty!
[*Although they continue to smile throughout this
scene, their voices grow steadily more biting
and their manner more irritated.*]

PERCINET.

Duty, and the Main Chance,—these two parks
and the farms—.

SYLVETTE.

So excellent! So wise! Who'd sigh for love's
alarms ?
—Yes; 'neath that wall our idyl's buried deep.

PERCINET.

There is no idyl left.

SYLVETTE.

I'm one now of the heap
Of dutiful young girls.

PERCINET.

Wed, wed in open mart.
—It was as Romeo that I won your heart!

SYLVETTE.

That you were Romeo—once—we'd best forget.

PERCINET.

My dear, you don't still think you're Juliet?

SYLVETTE.

You're growing—bitter.

PERCINET.

You—a trifle sour.

SYLVETTE.

If you're absurd, good heavens! have *I* power
To save you from it?

PERCINET.

If I was—absurd—
Was I the only one?

SYLVETTE.

All that's occurred
Is past and done.—But ah! my poor Blue Rose,
I've seen your petals drop. [*Maliciously.*] Drop
like those pseudo-foes!

PERCINET

[*sneering*].

That imitation rape!

SYLVETTE.

My hero—done in plaster !

PERCINET.

Abduction—as per bill !

SYLVETTE

[*with concentrated rage*].

Oh ! it was *all* disaster !
Our poetry was sham ; and, as soap-bubbles rise
And shine, and glow and burst before poor
                                    children's eyes,
So are we left abashed, and clutching soapy air !

PERCINET.

O great dead Loves,—great Loves,—whose fame
                         we sought to share !
You, whom I copied ; She, whose trailing dress
Was Sylvia's mantle once.   O noble Loveliness !
Pale, great Immortals !—we are less than naught.
You gave your royal love, but ours——

SYLVETTE

[*interrupting*].

Was taxed and bought !

PERCINET.

Instead of acting in some dream divine,
We've played burlesque, it seems.

SYLVETTE.

Yes, all the time.
Our nightingale was but a cackling goose !

PERCINET.

Our wall—my wall I vowed to such immortal use,
Was but a puppet-stand, a stage whereon each
day
We climbed and strutted, just as puppets may !
We posed as angels there—spread dazzling
wings,
And, all the time, our fathers worked the strings !

SYLVETTE.

Alas !—And yet [*thoughtfully*] still more gro-
tesque we'd be
If we ceased loving.

PERCINET.

Let's love furiously !
And, to begin with, we're compelled to love.

SYLVETTE.

But—we adore each other.

PERCINET.

That's what we must prove.

SYLVETTE

[*with forced amiability*].

'Tis only love could make us bear this blow ;
Is it not,—treasure ?

PERCINET

[*same manner*].

Angel ! it is so.

SYLVETTE

[*growing ironical*].

Good-bye, then, dearest Soul !

PERCINET

[*same manner*].

My only Joy, adieu !

SYLVETTE.

I 'll dream of you, dear Heart !

PERCINET.

Dear Heart ! I 'll dream of you.

SYLVETTE

[*snappishly*].

I go away—to dream.

PERCINET

[*same manner*].

I leave you—just to muse.

SYLVETTE

[*recovering herself enough to smile at him*].

Good night!

PERCINET.

Good-bye!   [*Same manner.*]

[*Exit* SYLVETTE.]

PERCINET

[*looks after her a moment, then says with an air of determined rage*].

My temper I won't lose!

[*After a pause; increasing bitterness.*]

—*She* treat me thus?   [*Enter* STRAFOREL, *who slowly and majestically comes down stage.*]   But who is yonder wight

In curious small clothes and huge mantle dight,

This much moustachioed, swagg'ring cavalier?

[*To* STRAFOREL, *after contemplating him in silence.*]

What is it?

STRAFOREL

[*smiling*].

A small reckoning brings me here.

PERCINET

[*impertinently*].

A tradesman ?

STRAFOREL

[*still smiling, bows mockingly*].

It would seem so.

[*With a change of manner to patronage.*]

PERCINET

[*losing all control*].

What! *you* here?   *You!*
[*He recovers himself and speaks with cold fury.*]
                              Sir! it is very well.—
It is not to be borne.—

STRAFOREL

[*smiling*].

So ho! the dear boy guesses?

PERCINET

[*throws at him the bill, which he draws all
crumpled out of his pocket*].

Ruffian—take that!

STRAFOREL

[*disdainfully*].

                    Dear child, avoid excesses!
[*Strikes new attitude.*]   I say, I'm Straforel.

PERCINET.

        Kind Heaven, that sent this man!
Why, I would range the earth——

STRAFOREL

[*complacently, interrupting*].

> That were a lengthy plan.

[*Mocking.*]

Quell that remorse, dear boy ; the victims whom
you slay

Are not in desperate case. [*Laughing.*] Behold *me*!

PERCINET

[*savagely, between his teeth*].

> There's a way !

[*He draws his sword and rushes at* STRAFOREL
furiously. STRAFOREL *does not draw his
sword but defends himself with his arm, as
easily and securely as a fencing-master giving
a lesson to a beginner.*]

STRAFOREL.

Up !—up that wrist !—That foot more back.—A
shame

At your age—to ignore—the—simplest fencing
—game.

[*He defends himself between the words, and disarms*
PERCINET. *He hands him back his sword
with an exaggerated bow.*]

What ! is your lesson over ?　Won't you play ?

PERCINET

[*humiliated, beside himself with rage*].

Oh, I am but a schoolboy; but——

[*with a sudden revulsion of feeling*]

Nay, nay,
I'll have—*revenge*! [*He seizes the sword.*]
I'll have my own affairs!
I'll drink and dice and brawl until the whole
world stares!
Don Juan's shade shall blush,—I'll love the ballet-
corps!

[*He runs off the stage brandishing his sword.*]

STRAFOREL

[*good-naturedly*].

Nice boy! But who the deuce is now to pay
my score?

[*A sound of furious quarrelling is heard off stage.*]
[STRAFOREL *peering behind the scenes.*]

What's that? Who's there? Who——

[*He bursts into violent laughter.*]

Save us, Heavenly Powers!

[*Enter* BERGAMIN *and* PASQUIN *in disorder, with-
out their wigs, their clothes all torn as after
a combat.*]

PASQUIN

[*readjusting his dress and handing* BERGAMIN *his
    wig. In a breathless voice, with immense
    dignity*].
There is your wig, sir.

BERGAMIN

[*half choked*].
                    Sir, I give you yours.

PASQUIN.

You understand that after such a scene—.
There is your ruffle.   [*Gives him torn ruffle.*]

[*Enter the* NOTARY *for the wedding contract, and the* WITNESSES *in their finest attire.*]

BERGAMIN

[*losing his head*].
The witnesses ?—the notary ?—Devils !

WITNESSES

[*scandalised*].

Hey ?

NOTARY

[*shocked and pompous*].
Such words to me !
[STRAFOREL, *in the midst of the uproar, has picked up and smoothed out the bill thrown at him by* PERCINET.]

STRAFOREL

[*thrusting the paper in* BERGAMIN'S *face*].
Pay me ;—in guineas ;—eighty-nine.
[*Enter the wedding-guests and three fiddlers playing a minuet.*]

BERGAMIN

[*beside himself, shoving people about*].
O devils ! Fiddles ! Devils ! [*To* STRAFOREL.] I decline
To listen. [*With explosion.*] Devils !
[*The fiddlers continue playing automatically.*]

STRAFOREL

[*impatiently to* BERGAMIN.]
Sir, sir! will you answer that? [*Indicates paper.*]

BERGAMIN.

Ask Pasquin.

PASQUIN.

No! ask *him*! [*Indicating* BERGAMIN.]

STRAFOREL.

What! shall I hold my hat?
[*He reads with emphasis the words of the bill:*]
'*One false rape, set in action to betroth*——'

BERGAMIN.

They're *not* betrothèd, and their broken oath
Breaks off your bargain.

STRAFOREL

[*to* PASQUIN].
Sir!

PASQUIN

[*protesting*].
                              Why should *I* pay
Now all is ended? [*Pettishly.*] Hang you! go
                                              away!

[BLAISE, *who enters, speaks apart
to* BERGAMIN.]

BERGAMIN

[*overcome*].

My son has left me !

SYLVETTE

[*taken aback*].

Gone ?

[STRAFOREL, *who was going up stage, stops short
and looks at her attentively.*]

STRAFOREL.

Hallo— ?

BERGAMIN.

Oh, fly
After him !   Quick !

[*He runs off stage, followed by the* NOTARY
and the wedding-guests.]

SYLVETTE

[*with deep emotion*].

Gone !

[STRAFOREL, *coming back and watching her.*]

STRAFOREL

[*aside*].

Is it writ that I
Shall bring these lambs together, in one fold ?

SYLVETTE

[*with sudden fury of indignation*].

Gone ?   No ; that is *too* much !
[*Exit, followed by* PASQUIN.]

STRAFOREL

[*triumphantly*].

Cheer up, my boy !   Behold,
If you would earn the guineas of your bill,
Here are two lovers, to be dealt with still !
[*Exit.   The three fiddlers, left alone in the middle
of the stage, continue to play their minuet.*]

CURTAIN.

END OF ACT II.

ACT III

SAME SCENE. *Materials for the rebuilding of the wall lie scattered about. Heaps of lime. Workmen's tools.*

BERGAMIN *and* PASQUIN, *each on a different side, are inspecting the work. A* MASON *is working at the wall, kneeling with his back to the audience.*

THE MASON

[*singing as he works*].

Fol-lol-de-ri-do !

BERGAMIN

[*discontentedly*].
 All workmen are so slow.

THE MASON.

Fol-lol-de-ri-do !

PASQUIN

[*watching him with satisfaction*].
 That's where the new bricks go !

BERGAMIN

Ha! now a touch of plaster!

PASQUIN.

Ho! now a splash of lime!

THE MASON

[*singing in operatic fashion*].
De ri-do! De ri-do! De ri, de ri, de ri-i-i-i-me!

PASQUIN.

Good voice.   The work is bad.
[*He comes down stage.*]

BERGAMIN

[*coming down stage, speaks with aggressive
cheerfulness*].
Ha, ha! and now—look here,
My wall is well begun.

PASQUIN

[*stamping upon the spot where the wall is down*].
To-morrow noon, 'tis clear,
My wall will count two feet—two feet of wall,
by Jove!

BERGAMIN

[*in a lyric outburst*].

Wall of *my* dreams, arise ! arise and be my love !

PASQUIN

[*sharply*].

Did you speak, sir ?

BERGAMIN

[*with dignity*].

I spoke.   [*Sneering.*]   I hope I have
the right ?   [*A pause.*]

BERGAMIN

[*abruptly, confidentially*].

Ahem ! . . . How go the cards ? Who plays
with you at night ?

PASQUIN

[*drearily*].

No one.   And you ?

BERGAMIN

I ? No one.

[*A pause. They bow ceremoniously to one
another and walk about.*]

PASQUIN
[*standing still*].
You've not heard
News of your son ?

BERGAMIN.
No.   Nothing.

PASQUIN
[*politely*].
Not a word ?
'Pon my faith, neighbour, thieves will pluck him
close
Ere *he* returns !

BERGAMIN.
I thank you.

PASQUIN
[*chuckling*].
Ah, boys, boys !
[*They salute one another and walk about.   A pause.*]

PASQUIN
[*stopping short*].
Now that my sheltering wall stands firm once
more,
I don't object—.   [*He hesitates.*]—I don't *forbid*
my door.
Come in—sometimes—to see me.

BERGAMIN

[*stiffly*].

When I choose I'll come.

[*They bow ceremoniously.*]

PASQUIN

[*abruptly*].

I say, come now.   The cards are laid at home.

BERGAMIN

[*hesitating*].

But can I?—I don't know.—I have not under-
stood——

PASQUIN.

But—since the cards are laid!

[*Coaxingly.*]

One cribbage to the good.

BERGAMIN

[*with dignity*].

I'd rather play bezique.

PASQUIN.

Come quick!

[*He turns to go.*]

BERGAMIN

[*following him*].

You owe me still——

PASQUIN

[*waving his hand to the* MASON].

Work well, my man!

THE MASON

[*at the top of his voice*].
Tra-*la*!

BERGAMIN

[*patronisingly*].

Fine voice that, if you will!
[*Exeunt. As they go off the stage the* MASON
turns round and takes off his hat, revealing
STRAFOREL.]

STRAFOREL

[*imitating* PASQUIN'S *voice*].

Work well, my man!
His man! work well! ha! ha! and all
Because I'm come, disguised, to furbish up their
wall!

[*He sits down upon the unfinished piece of wall.*]

The youngster's still afield; still gaping after
fame.

[*Shrugging his shoulders.*]

It needs no magic glass to follow out *that* game!
Prodigal sons return.   We'll leave him for a
day,
For life—great Mistress Life—to teach him her
own way;
To douse him with chill facts; to clip his wand'ring
wing,
And send him whimpering home.   Meanwhile, I
sit and sing,
Plotting to cure fair Sylvia of her craze
For new adventure.   In the golden days
When I went ruffling through the country towns,
Squand'ring my wits on thick-head louts and
clowns,
I often played the duke; 'tis but a marquis now,
So at it, boy, and——

[*he draws a letter from his doublet, and hides it
in the mossy trunk of a tree*]

Ha!   These fathers, you'll allow,
Do owe me——

[*seeing* SYLVETTE *approach*]

Why, 'tis she, the fair fantastic may!

[*He seizes his trowel and disappears behind the
wall.* SYLVETTE *appears.   She looks about
her furtively, making sure she is not watched.*]

H

SYLVETTE.

Nobody !—and my letter ?

[*She lays her muslin mantle on a bench, etc.*]

Day by day

[*she goes to the tree*]

Some gallant—some adorer—some unseen
Beautiful lover, brings—

[*she plunges her hand into the tree-trunk, and
holds up letter*]

A flower i' the green !

[*She reads aloud.*]

'O Sylvia, Sylvia, marble-hearted, quite !
'This is the last'—

[*she looks up*]

—The last ?—'complaining I indite.
'What ! still no answer, tiger-hearted maid ?
'What ! still no pity ?' [*Spoken.*]   Oh, I am
afraid !

[*Reads.*]

'Love in my hollow heart reverberates forlorn'—
[*Spoken.*]

How well he writes !

[*She crumples up the paper nervously.*]

And Percinet—is gone !
He left me for the world.   I 'll do as much for him.
I will not wait alone and watch my dreams grow
dim.

—Let him but claim me now, this lord who loves
me so—.

[*She looks at the letter.*]

'O tiger-hearted maid!' Alas! how should men
know?

From out these dull green leaves, all full of nests
and birds,

Let him appear, like dawn, and claim me with
sweet words—

With strange, sweet words. And, as I am—un-
curled,

Without a hat—I'd fly, I'd follow round the world!

[*Holding out her hands.*]

Whatever it may cost, break, custom's iron bands!

My lover, still unknown, see! I stretch suppliant
hands.

Where art thou?

[*Enter* STRAFOREL.]

STRAFOREL

[*in a loud voice*].

Here!

SYLVETTE.

O help! O help me, Percinet!

[*Going backwards as* STRAFOREL *advances.*]

How dare you, sir, come near!

STRAFOREL

[*in a lover-like voice*].

What ! send your slave away ?
—Mine was the letter, sweet, you read but now.
I am that favoured mortal, whose rash vow
You hearkened and approved.   And mine the
rapturous plan
To carry off my bride——

SYLVETTE

[*bewildered*].

How—dare you speak so—*man* !

STRAFOREL.

A man ?—you take me for a *man*, sweet miss ?
Now, stap my vitals ! what a jest is this !
[*He speaks with a grand air.*]
Your servant still, though lord of many lands,
The Marquess D'Astafiorquercita stands,
Your lover here confessed. [*Strikes attitude.*]   His
sad, sick heart
Long since despaired of Peace. [*Confidentially.*]
That is a part
Of all romance.—Yet, on the other hand,
His life is wild, and terrible, and grand.
He 's a knight-errant.   He 's a poet, too—
A marquis ;—and he wields this tool [*brandishes
trowel*] for you !
[*He throws his trowel away with an elegant air,*

and tearing off his linen coat and white hat, covered with lime, appears in a brilliant, fantastic costume, fair curling wig, military moustache.]

SYLVETTE
[*startled*].

My lord——

STRAFOREL
[*interrupting*].

For love it was, for love of you, I came.
A certain Straforel once spoke your charming
name ;—
Since then I 'm mad with love—quite mad—afire,
I swear,
To right your cruel wrongs——

SYLVETTE
[*bewildered*].

I know not what they were !

STRAFOREL.

Angels forget; but I—nay, do not tremble, Sweet,
For Straforel is dead—I slew him at my feet.

SYLVETTE
[*horrified*].

You killed him !

STRAFOREL

[*showing his hand*].

With this hand.   It always was my joy
To kill my fellow-man.
[*He curls his moustache.   Complacently.*]
I 've practised since a boy.

SYLVETTE.

Merciful Heaven ! my·lord !

STRAFOREL

[*patronisingly*].

Leave all to me, fair Flower—
At any cost you crave to live one royal hour.

SYLVETTE

[*protesting*].

My lord !

STRAFOREL.

My word is pledged.   To-night I claim my wife.

SYLVETTE.

O sir !

STRAFOREL.

I 'm not in jest.

SYLVETTE.

My lord !

STRAFOREL.

My Dearest Life !
But you are deeply pledged.   I heard you speak
the words.
At dusk we'll fly away—we two—like frighted
birds, [*with a swaggering air*]
And if your worthy merchant-father lose his head
With grief—such things have been——

SYLVETTE

[*piteously*].

My lord !

STRAFOREL.

Nay, strike me dead !
It were a merry jest.   I'll shoot men on our
track
Like dogs ; since, once eloped, there is no turning
back.
Ho for a merry life !

SYLVETTE

[*frightened*].

But, sir——

STRAFOREL.

The life for me !
Say, Sweetheart, shall we fly when winds and
storms are free ?
When on our naked heads the wild rains beat——

SYLVETTE
[*alarmed*].

O sir !

STRAFOREL.

The paths of joy are red from bleeding feet.

SYLVETTE
[*piteously*].

But, sir !

STRAFOREL.

In unknown lands, far from all human ken,
We'll live in lone content, dressed like two
beggar-men.

SYLVETTE
[*startled*].

But why ?

STRAFOREL
[*proudly*].

I have no gold. [*Scornfully.*] You would
not have me—*rich* ?

SYLVETTE

[*doubtfully*].

I——

STRAFOREL

[*patronisingly*].

'Love me for myself.' *I* know.   Don't blush,
sweet witch !

[*Declaiming.*]

Once there, we'll live on crusts—crusts soaked
in lovers' tears.

SYLVETTE

[*horrified*].

My lord——!

STRAFOREL.

We'll live alone, and all forgot, for years.

SYLVETTE

[*protesting*].

But I——

STRAFOREL.

Not in a house.   No, we shall find content
In simpler things than *that.*   I'll love you in a
tent.

SYLVETTE.

A tent !

STRAFOREL.

Ropes, canvas, tent-poles, six or seven—
[*declaiming*]
The only bars between us and high heaven.

SYLVETTE

[*aghast*].

What have I done ?

STRAFOREL

[*tenderly*].
What ! still a-quaking, Sweet ?
You fear the road is long for such small feet ?
So be it.   We will hide, my fairest Queen,
Wherever we may hope to live unseen.
O solitude—O rapture——

SYLVETTE

[*timidly*].
You mistake——

STRAFOREL.

Never an honest man this guilty hand will take.
What matter ?

SYLVETTE.

Matter !

STRAFOREL.

Prejudice, my Own.
This world was only built to be o'erthrown.
Our happiness shall spring from our disgrace.

SYLVETTE
[*with dignity*].

My lord !

STRAFOREL.

All day I'll contemplate your face.
My only task, to hymn your praise in song——

SYLVETTE
[*deprecating*].

My lord——

STRAFOREL.

O Poesy, O Passion !—All day long.—
Then, I'll be jealous of your slightest look——

SYLVETTE
[*protesting*].

My lord !

STRAFOREL.

Like black Othello in the story-book,
I'll howl like wolves, like jackals, and like bears——

SYLVETTE

[*falls half fainting on the bench*].

My lord !

STRAFOREL.

I 'll drown you in your own salt tears,
If you but rattle at your chains.

SYLVETTE

[*faintly*].

My lord !

STRAFOREL

[*with a magnificent air*].
The chains of love are sacred, my Adored.

SYLVETTE

[*taking courage*].

My lord——

STRAFOREL

[*menacing*].
You tremble ?

SYLVETTE

[*relapsing*].
Heaven ! those awful chains.

STRAFOREL

[*snatching at her hand violently*].

Does milk and water blue these lovely veins?

[*He kisses her hand and throws it aside.*]

Are you a schoolgirl thus to shrink from me?—
Shrink from your high, romantic destiny?
See, now I go; [*threateningly*] but shall I go—
beguiled?

SYLVETTE

[*faltering*].

My lord——

STRAFOREL

[*patronisingly*].

I understand.   Comfort your soul, my
child!
To-night, this very night, upon my wildest horse
I'll bear you far away.   You'll suffer, dear, of
course,
But sedan chairs are slow—are slow and very
dear;
And *this* elopement counts.   I'll come for you,
no fear.

[*Goes up stage.*]

SYLVETTE

[*faintly*].

My lord——!

STRAFOREL

I shall return.

SYLVETTE

[*imploringly*].
My lord!

STRAFOREL

[*waving his hand*].
I come again.
Let me but seek my cloak, my steed with tossing
mane.

SYLVETTE

[*imploringly*].
My lord!

STRAFOREL

[*waving his arms with a magnificent gesture*].
And we shall fly from distant shore to shore.
[*Comes down stage.*]
O dearest dream of love! O heart that beats
once more!
Sweet soul! to whom my soul can whisper—'Lo!
my bride!'
I shall return, to stay——

SYLVETTE

[*in a half-choked voice*].
To stay?

STRAFOREL.

Yes ; by thy side
To live for evermore — to live while worlds
endure.
[*Fatuously.*]
You loved me ere we met. We met. My love
was sure.—
[*Before going out he turns and sees her half
fainting on the bench. Aside.*]
Flourish of trumpets ; enter Percinet !
[*Exit.*]

SYLVETTE

[*opening her eyes ; faintly*].

My lord ! O sir ! Oh, not—not in that awful
way !
Oh pity me, my lord !—*Not* on the champing
steed.
Let me go home instead. I could not bear—
Indeed.
A schoolgirl.—That is all. My lord !—I would
not seem
Anything more. My lord !
[*She looks about her.*]
Gone ? What an *awful* dream !
[*A pause. She sits up and collects herself.*]

I'd rather serious things would happen but in
jest.

[*She gets up.*]

O Sylvia, O my dear, this thing you held for
best,

This love you longed to know—this lover heaven-
sent—

Oh!—

[*She throws up her arms.*]

Beggars' clothes and scorn ;—exile—and oh, that
tent !

Alas ! he brought too much.   Ah me, I wanted
less :

A laurel leaf or two dropped in the daily mess ;

—Not bitterness of bays—but spice to daily
meat.

[*She sighs pensively.*]

I could be happy now with something—not so
sweet.—

[*The twilight deepens in the park.   She takes up
her muslin veil left on the bench and covers
her head and shoulders with it.   She murmurs
dreamily.*]

Who knows ?

[*Enter* PERCINET.   *He is in rags, his arm in a
sling ; he drags himself with difficulty.   His
hat, in which the feather is broken, nearly
conceals his face.*   SYLVETTE *has not yet
seen him.*]

PERCINET.

Since yester morn I have not broken bread,
Nor eat, nor drank, nor slept ; and oh, this throb-
bing head !
—O sorry, sorry sport !—Farewell, adventures
all !
Mine ears are leaden grown when syren voices
call.

[*He leans upon the wall, his hat falls and uncovers his face.* SYLVETTE *catches sight of him.*]

SYLVETTE.

You ?
[*He springs up aghast. She looks at him.*]
And in what a plight ! Oh ! can it——

PERCINET
[*grimly*].

It *can* be.
—The Prodigal's Return.—[*Piteously.*] Alas, alas
for me !

[*He staggers.*]

SYLVETTE
[*clasping her hands*].

Alack ! he 's fain to fall !

PERCINET

[*reassuringly*].

Nothing ; a passing thrill——

SYLVETTE

[*catching sight of his arm, and with a cry*].

Wounded !

PERCINET

[*quickly*].

And can your heart forgive, O Sylvia, still ?

SYLVETTE

[*severely, moving away*].

Only a father, sir, the fatted calf should slay.
[PERCINET *makes a quick movement, and his
wounded arm makes him wince.*]

SYLVETTE

[*speaking involuntarily, alarmed*].

Alas, that wound !

PERCINET

[*sadly*].

Alas ! for poorest Percinet !
Yet spare your sweetest tears ; I would not have
you grieve.

SYLVETTE

[*childishly*].

Where were you all this time ?   How could you
                                        bear to leave
She—those you love, I mean ?

PERCINET

[*shaking his head*].
            Sylvette, I wrought no good.
[*He coughs.*]

SYLVETTE

[*quickly*].

And now that cruel cough——

PERCINET

[*shaking his head*].
                If you but understood !
[*Mysteriously.*]
Roaming afar, at night——

SYLVETTE

[*ingenuously*].

            And *that's* how men catch cold !
—How strangely you are dressed !

PERCINET.

Alas! must you be told ?
—How among thieves I fell, and grovelled among
swine ?

SYLVETTE

[*ironically*].

That's Life.   *I've* learned that too.
[*With ill-repressed curiosity.*]
Were the strange ladies fine ?

PERCINET

[*hastily*].

Don't talk of them, my dear.

SYLVETTE.

And on high balconies,
With silken ladders hung, did you ascend the
skies ?

PERCINET
[*aside*].

I nearly broke my neck !

SYLVETTE
[*ironically*].

Oh brave, whom love inspires !

PERCINET

[*aside*].

Alas, poor silly sheep, with coat torn by the
briars !

SYLVETTE.

Long in your memory will such great hours stay !

PERCINET

[*aside*].

How in a cupboard hid I spent one summer day.

SYLVETTE.

The gallant wagers won——

PERCINET.

Oh. yes, oh yes ; [*aside*] and how
An angry spouse belabours
[*He rubs his shoulder.*]

SYLVETTE

[*admiringly, pointing to his arm*].

Wounded now ?

PERCINET

[*aside*].

It nearly cost my life.

SYLVETTE

[*doubtfully*].

And yet you have come back?

PERCINET.

Athirst; afoot; stripped bare; a sorry sight,
alack!

SYLVETTE

[*enthusiastically*].

Yes; but at least you 've seen, you 've found True
Poetry!

PERCINET.

I sought it far and wide.
[*He speaks tenderly.*]
I left it, dear, with thee.
Ah, do not mock me, Sweet, dear Sweet whom I
adore!

SYLVETTE.

Alas, 'tis *you* forget! Alas, those days are o'er!

PERCINET.

But why?

SYLVETTE

[*sadly*].

You have forgot. *They* held us up to scorn.

PERCINET.

They? ·Who? [*Aside.*] My heart awakes; it
wakes to shining dawn!

SYLVETTE.

Our fathers played at hate.

PERCINET

[*quickly*].
  We played at love's delight.

SYLVETTE

[*shaking her head*].
Oh, that's all very well. *I've* not forgotten,
quite!
[*With reproach.*]
You called this wall a stage where silly puppets
played.

PERCINET

[*embarrassed*].
I said—I did not say——
[*with an outburst*]
—What matter what I said?

Dear wall, dear stage, dear mossy stage leaf-set!
With great green boughs for screens, and heaven
                                        for parapet.
            [He *points with his hand.*]
Our   backcloth   this   old   park,   that   fades   to
                                    tenderest blue;
The flaming sun for lamp; and Juliet played by
                                            you;
Where   winds   breathe   discourse   sweet,   where
                            flowers and sun and birds
Act the old play for which our Shakespeare made
                                        the words.
Yes . . . though our fathers bade us speak the
                                            parts,
Pulled   puppet-strings,   and   thought   to   tutor
                                            hearts—
It was a stage, my Sylvia, where the play
Had been rehearsed by Love—by Love!

                    SYLVETTE.

                            Alack the day!
But we were guilty, or we thought it guilt.

                    PERCINET

            [*reassuringly*].

Guilty we were.   A crime is always built
On bad intentions; and we *meant* a crime,
And so are sinners——

SYLVETTE

[*doubtfully*].

But that other time——

PERCINET

[*quickly*].

Sinners !—I would not rob you of one pang.
For less than this men have been doomed to hang.

SYLVETTE.

You swear it ?   [*She looks doubtful.*]

PERCINET

[*fervently*].

By your sweet, your balmy breath !
We have been guilty, love, guilty to death.

SYLVETTE

[*shaken in her conviction, sitting down quite near him*].

Really guilty ?   [*Gets up and moves away.*]   Yet,
O Percinet,
Our danger was not danger—it was play.

PERCINET.

It was true danger if we held it true.

SYLVETTE

[*sadly*].

That rape was but a seeming; even you—
Your rescue was the merest fairy-tale.

PERCINET.

Were you less frightened? Did you turn less
pale?
And since your soul has tasted the rude woe
Of an abduction, I would have you know
It is the same, my love, as if you'd fled.

SYLVETTE

[*shaking her head*].

No; the dear dream is spoilt, the charm is sped.
Those masks, those cloaks, that music i' the night,
That thrilling combat—for I saw you fight!
[*Clasping her hands.*]
I saw you as a god, whose victims fell.
[*Pouting.*]
Yet all was feigned, by Master Straforel!

PERCINET.

And could he feign that night of Paradise,
That lovely gift of April to our love?—
Or set with stars the starry shining skies?
Or teach the mist to shimmer like a dove?

Was it his power that bade the roses dim
Float in mid-air, like flowers on a stream,
Till, like a redder rose, above the rim
Of dreaming woods, the moon rose in our dream ?

SYLVETTE.

O Percinet !

PERCINET.

O love ! young as that night of spring,
A-fire with youth ; a-bloom ; untouched ; in-
                                        violate ;—
What need of magic here ?   O fond Heart,
                                    wavering,
Fly to your nest at last.   My dove has found her
                                        mate !

SYLVETTE

[*with emotion*].

Your dove ?   [*She turns away and sheds tears.*]

PERCINET.

A tear ?   [*He takes her by the hand.*]
          A pearl ?   [*Kissing her hand.*]
                You can forgive me—so ?

SYLVETTE

[*simply*].

I loved you all the while.   I think I did not know.

Percinet.

This is your brow; this is your lovely hair;
The virgin breath of you makes sweet this
                                        night;
The angels in God's heaven are not more fair.
  [*He plays with her floating veil.*]
Oh, let me kiss this hem of maiden white!
Come! blessèd cloud, my dear love's dearest veil!
Come, cool my parchèd lips with thy perfumes!
  [Half aside.]
How could I slight these maiden muslins pale
For all the silks and velvets of their looms?

Sylvette

  [*quickly, with curiosity*].
What silk? Whose velvet?

Percinet.

                    No one, O my Sweet!
My child; my Sylvia; at your sacred feet
  [*he kneels*]
I kneel to worship Whiteness.

Sylvette

  [*looking down*].
                    My poor dress
Is only linen, dearest.

PERCINET.

See, I press
My lips upon its border, bending low
Lest I should soil my sweet saint's robe of
snow.

This linen fold
That clips you tight,
As envious clouds enfold
The light ;

This thin white lawn—
White flutterings,
Outspread, indrawn—
Your wings ;

This linen fold
So seemly laid—
A look, overbold,
Might fade ;

This filmy lawn—
As virginally fair
As the cobweb, born
'Mid air ;

This linen fold—
As dainty-bright
As are your thoughts, untold,
All white ;

This speckless lawn—
Dazzling like snow, like fire—
The soul of You ; withdrawn
From my desire ;

White folds below, above—
White veils where I adore,—
White veils of You!   What should I love
Or worship more?

SYLVETTE.

Oh, not in distant lands, in untrod ways,
In wild adventure or in unsung lays,
But *here* lives Poetry!

[*She falls into his arms.*]

PERCINET

[*shaking his head*].

I cannot praise at all
My own adventures as poetical.

SYLVETTE.

The storms our fathers planned were fruitful
showers:
They shook our souls, but brought our love to
light.

PERCINET.

What though the web was false? the golden
flowers
Were 'broidered there by love for our delight.

SYLVETTE.

O foolish, foolish, foolish girl and boy
To seek for joy and love, when we are Love and
Joy !

[*Enter* STRAFOREL. *He recalls the fathers and
shows them* SYLVETTE *and* PERCINET *in one
another's arms.*]

STRAFOREL.

Look !   Reconciled !

BERGAMIN.

My son !   [*He embraces* PERCINET.]

STRAFOREL.

You 'll pay me now ?

PASQUIN

[*to his daughter*].

You love the boy again ?

SYLVETTE.

Yes.

PASQUIN.

Lord ! a woman's vow !

STRAFOREL.

I 'll get my well-earned gold ?

BERGAMIN.

You 'll get both gold and glory.

SYLVETTE

[*startled*].

That voice ? O Heavens !—The Marquis of my
story !

STRAFOREL

[*bowing*].

Your Marquis ?   It was I, most charming Miss,
I—Straforel !—Forgive me, that in this
My zeal forestalled your wishes, and I took
Means just to give you, in a single look,
That knowledge women often travel far
To find out for themselves—how dull adventures
are !
Doubtless you too, like him, [*indicating* PERCINET]
our dear young friend,
Might find this out in time ; but, faith ! that
bitter end
Is far to seek.   The world is hard and wide.

[*Confidentially.*]

I showed you my best magic-lantern slide !

PERCINET.

What's that?

SYLVETTE
[*hastily*].
Nothing.   I love you!

BERGAMIN
[*pointing to the wall begun*].
And to-morrow—bang!
Down with those stones, and let all walls go
hang!

PASQUIN.
Away with all that ever stands between!

STRAFOREL.
No; keep your walls.   Without them naught had
been.

SYLVETTE
[*summoning the actors about her*].
And now we five—if Master Straforel please—
Let us expound the play in which we've tried to
please.

[*She comes down stage and addresses the audience,
marking time with her hand.*]

Light, easy rhymes; old dresses, frail and light;
Love in a park, fluting an ancient tune.
[*Soft music.*]
K

BERGAMIN.

A fairy-tale quintet, mad as Midsummer-night.

PASQUIN.

Some quarrels.   Yes !—but all so very slight !

STRAFOREL.

Madness of sunstroke ; madness of the moon !
A worthy villain, in his mantle dight.

SYLVETTE.

Light, easy rhymes ; old dresses, frail and light ;
Love in a park, fluting an ancient tune.

PERCINET.

A Watteau picture—not by Watteau, quite ;
Release from many a dreary Northern rune ;
Lovers and fathers ; old walls, flowery-bright ;
A brave old plot—with music—ending soon.

SYLVETTE.

Light, easy rhymes ; old dresses, frail and light.

[*The stage gradually darkens ; the last lines are
     delivered in voices that grow fainter as the
     actors appear to fade away into mist and
     darkness.*]

CURTAIN.

THE END.

Edinburgh : T. and A. CONSTABLE, Printers to Her Majesty